S0-AXO-363

GET BACK TO

BEAUTIFUL

By Katrina M. Henderson

ROYSTON
Publishing

BK Royston Publishing
P. O. Box 4321
Jeffersonville, IN 47131
502-802-5385
http://www.bkroystonpublishing.com
bkroystonpublishing@gmail.com

© Copyright – 2018

All Rights Reserved. No part of this book may be reproduced, stored in a retrieval system, or transmitted by any means without the written permission of the author.

Cover Design: Kamal Designs
Photographer Credit for Author Picture:
Jermoni Dowd JKDowd Media, LLC

ISBN: 978-1-946111-48-7

Printed in the United States of America

ACKNOWLEDGMENTS

Thank you to everyone who has believed in me on my journey to encouraging others! I dedicate this book to all my family and friends who have pushed me in some way or another to keep doing what God has gifted within me. It hasn't been easy but I kept pushing!

To my children, Kaila, Arianna and Nicholas, I want you to know and believe that you should never stop dreaming. Never stop pushing for what you believe! Never stop pushing to serve God! You are going to walk in your own journeys and I want you to know that I am with you every step of the way. Every day I am blessed to experience your greatness and you are so awesome! I love you with everything in my body! Do not and I mean do not, let someone tell you that you can't. If you believe you can, then make it happen and it will be done! Show the world who God created you to be! Continue to live in your freedom and activate your greatness!

To my mother, Lisa, thank you for being my biggest supporter! You may not have always agreed with my decisions but you let them be my "decisions".

To my husband, Andre, thank you for showing me it's ok to be me! Your love and dedication to this family is far more than I could have ever imagined. Thank you for supporting me in fulfilling my dreams!

To my Dad, thank you for being an example of work ethic. Your drive and determination for success is who I am today!

To my Coach, Dawniel Winningham, thank you for speaking life into me through your courses, webinars, and discussions! You showed me how to make it all come together and I am forever grateful!

Finally, as you already know, I am so thankful to God for blessing me the way He has! He told me what to do and this book is a result of me carrying that out! If I can do it, you can too!

TABLE OF CONTENTS

INTRODUCTION

Get Back to Beautiful came out of a conversation that I had with a young woman when she wanted to order a shirt for her birthday. I suggested the Birthday Beauty shirt but she said she felt self-conscious about calling herself beautiful. My response was that's the reason why you need to order it!

Who said we can't call ourselves beautiful? Why do people think we are conceited or all about ourselves when we do? We were created to be beautiful but life happens and we dim our light. We let our obstacles tell us that we are not good enough and we begin to have self-doubt.

This book will require you to let go of your fears and past experiences in hopes of showing you the beauty within. On this journey, you will have a daily word of encouragement, affirmation, scripture, and a get back to beautiful assignment for the next 30 days! I'm challenging you to complete only one day at a time and pray/meditate on the experience to receive what God is giving you on this journey. Some days will be harder than others days because of the truths that will be revealed; however, I can tell you that freedom will come at the end. Beautiful, stay the course no matter what and get back to beautiful!

Day #1

Hi, Beautiful! Yes, I'm talking to you! Why wouldn't I be talking to you? What stops you from loving yourself? What stops you from saying you are beautiful? So many of us have allowed our past hurts and failures to define us and we have thought less of ourselves. We think we can't be beautiful because so and so didn't love me or because I didn't accomplish XYZ. We also think we can't be beautiful because of the way society defines beauty. They say we have to be the perfect size and shape.

My biggest question to you is - why did our past tell us we were not beautiful? Do those experiences tell us we are anything less than beautiful? No, they don't. They just told us that we are human and there was a lesson that we learned in the situation. From those experiences, we learned what we didn't want in a relationship or that job wasn't our purpose. So, we ultimately learned that we get to try again! But, no matter what, we should have never stopped loving ourselves, or thinking we are anything less than beautiful! Those events do not define our beauty! They may help shape who we are because of the lessons encountered but they don't tell us we are beautiful because God has told us that when He created us. So repeat after me, I am beautiful!

Affirmation: I am Beautiful because I am fearfully and wonderfully made!

Daily Scripture: I praise you because I am fearfully and wonderfully made; your works are wonderful, I know that full well. **Psalm 139:14 NIV**

Get Back to Beautiful Exercise: Stand in the mirror and say "**I am beautiful**" 10 times and journalize what you are feeling. Don't be afraid of the emotions that will come. Just take a leap and trust the process. You are beautiful and you need every negative thought to leave your mind until you realize and accept that you are beautiful! Repeat the affirmation as many times as needed! Let it all go and regain your beauty!

Day #2

Did you say your daily affirmation from yesterday? If so, I hope you feel empowered! If not, I pray that you try again.

We have to accept that we are not perfect but we are still beautiful! In addition, there is no one who can tell us otherwise! Sure, we will make mistakes but that's all that they are. They are pieces to the puzzle called life. At the time, those pieces didn't fit in the space we were trying to make them fit. God created us in His image and we have to accept that we are not perfect nor are we intended to be perfect! He is the only perfect one! Therefore, give yourself credit for what you've accomplished and continue believing for what you have yet to accomplish! Be thankful for the moment! God loves you with all your flaws and He continues to love you no matter what! So, start loving yourself unconditionally! Our beauty comes from our forgiveness of ourselves.

Affirmation: God loves me with my flaws and all so I love me with my flaws and all!

Daily Scripture: "You are altogether beautiful, my darling; there is no flaw in you." **Song of Solomon 4:7 NIV**

Get Back to Beautiful Exercise: Take a sheet of paper and divide the paper in half vertically. At the top of the left column, title it "Perceived Flaws" and on the right side, title it "God's View." On the left side, write a list of what you perceive your flaws to be. On the right side, write a statement of what God would say for that flaw. For example, flaw - I am overweight. God's view - I am created in His image and I will do the work to be healthy. The items on the left are just perceived because that's not what God thinks of you. He is your Creator and we have to learn to appreciate the beauty that He created. It's all about changing your perspective and the context behind the perceived flaw. God loves you with all your flaws and all!

Day #3

As women, we make so many sacrifices for others that it hinders our peace. We are naturally giving but how can we give if we are burnt out and don't practice self-love! Hmm, you have the screaming baby in your arms, trying to cook dinner, bills laid out at the table, and attempting to keep it all together at the same time! Oh, maybe that's just me! Although, he's not a baby anymore. LOL

No matter what your story is, you have to take care of yourself and make time for you. Make a commitment to do something for you, just for you! Finally say it's ok for me to be selfish because I'm worth it!

You are good enough not because of what you have or your profession, but because of whom God says you are!

Affirmation: I am a Gift and I deserve to treat myself like one!

<u>Daily Scripture:</u> I am a gift from God **Psalm 127:3**

<u>Get Back to Beautiful Exercise:</u> Go get a facial, massage, manicure and pedicure or do something as simple as a walk in the park and just observe your surroundings! Stop looking at your circumstances and start living! Admire all the ways God's creations flow together, admire the sound of laughter, and admire the beauty within you even if you are in a torn tee and sweatpants. You were created from His beauty and you are beautiful!

Day #4

Sometimes life throws us challenges that often leave us feeling breathless and wondering why me! We sit back and say why this time! We question every obstacle and wonder at what point enough is enough! I know life is hard and we sometimes feel like giving up, but just remember there is purpose on the other side of that challenge! There is a destiny waiting for you to get the lesson so you can share your testimony with someone else who may be going through something similar. Continue to push through and know that you are stronger than you ever know! He would not have brought you to it, if He wasn't going to bring you through it! Push through and fulfill your purpose!

Affirmation: I was born for this! I believe, I can and I will!

Daily Scripture: "She is clothed with strength and dignity, and she laughs without fear of the future." **Proverbs 31:25 NLT**

<u>Get Back to Beautiful Exercise:</u> Acknowledge and admire your inner beauty! Write down all the beauty that you give, do, and create which includes being a mother, friend, wife, teacher, cook, etc. Don't you see all that beauty that is within!

She Believed She Could So She Did

Day #5

Imagine you are in a workshop or class and the professor asks you to write down characteristics that describe yourself. If you are like me, it's easier to describe my weaknesses than my strengths. Why? Because of my fear of thinking, I'm not worthy enough! Well, guess what? I am and so are you! You were created for a purpose! You were created in His image so you are **absolutely** beautiful! A woman's confidence is everything when she doesn't look at her outward beauty but realizes the beauty of God's love within her. You can get through any and everything when you believe He has your back. You can do all things because He has already done it!

Affirmation: I am Enough! I am Worthy!

Daily Scripture: "I can do all things through Christ who strengthens me." **Philippians 4:13**

<u>Get Back to Beautiful Exercise:</u> What is the one compliment that you continually get? Now, stand in the mirror and say that to yourself 10 times, and write what you are feeling.

Day #6

Say it with me - I am Bold! I am Beautiful!

Often times, we sit and perceive ourselves as one way but never really reflect on who God says we are. We are changed by our life experiences and challenges and sometimes that leaves us feeling like we are weak and not beautiful! We develop low self-esteem and don't have real relationships because we are afraid of letting others get to know the real us. When I say real, I mean the real woman that **God** has called us to be. You can't let your hurt stop you from pursuing your purpose. Your beauty is found in your confidence! Therefore, pray to God for Him to reveal who we truly are. In our prayers, we have to be prepared for the journey and all the truth that is revealed. Therefore, when you hear God say, "be bold", you have to be bold regardless of what it looks or more importantly, what it feels like. He is with us every step of the way!

Affirmation: I am Bold! I am Beautiful!

Daily Scripture: "We demolish arguments and every pretension that sets itself up against the knowledge of God, and we take captive every thought to make it obedient to Christ." **2 Cor. 10:5 NIV**

Get Back to Beautiful Exercise: Close your eyes and quiet your mind. Visualize yourself through the eyes of God (your Creator) and write down what He reveals. Remember the hardest part of this exercise is quieting your mind. Stop listening to the negative that surrounds your mind but truly focus on what God is telling you. Focus on the beauty of our Creator and allow Him to show you how He sees your beauty. Change the arguments in your head to what He says! Take captive every thought and get your beauty back!

Day #7

Adversity can come to distract us or to create a roadblock to get us in another direction. Often times, we don't think of the adversity as part of God's plan but it actually could be a part of His plan. The challenges may be coming because we have different choices that need to be made. Either our choices will have us trying to figure it out ourselves, or the choices force us to let go and let God take control of the challenges. As women, we can do many things but we are often finding ourselves carrying more than what's intended. We think, "oh I got this" and we won't ask for help, or we sit and cry because it's too much! Well, the next time you are faced with a challenge, ask yourself "is this my burden to bear?" or are you picking up bricks that don't have your name on them and trying to build a foundation? Whatever the situation, you are not alone and you will get through this! No matter what goes on in your life, please make sure that you are pressing forward. Be encouraged! Now, throw some of those bricks back as they are not yours to carry!

Affirmation: I'm an Overcomer! I'm thankful for all my circumstances!

Daily Scripture: Always be joyful. Never stop praying. Be thankful in all circumstances, for this is God's will for you who belong to Christ Jesus. **1 Thessalonians 5:16-18 NLT**

Get Back to Beautiful Exercise: What are you thankful and grateful for? List five things you are thankful for daily, and reflect on those during the day and during the rough moments.

Day #8

What are your dreams and aspirations? What purpose do you want to fulfill in your life? For so long, I had been on a journey for my purpose and I finally walked in it about two years ago. Who knew that what came so easily would be what God turned into greater for His good! Of course, you have self-doubt and question what it is that you are supposed to be doing. We want this glamorous thing and never look at the obvious of what's been there the entire time. Stop overcomplicating things! (Ha! I'm telling myself this as I write.) Stop giving up on your dreams and remember you can do all things. You have to have greater faith like never before! See yourself accomplishing your dreams now and make a plan to get there! Visualizing and believing is everything! Faith defeats fear every time but you must do the work!

Affirmation: I believe in me! My purpose will be fulfilled!

<u>Daily Scripture:</u> Faith without works is dead! **James 2:14-26**

Don't fear, because I am with you; don't be afraid, for I am your God. I will strengthen you, I will surely help you; I will hold you with my righteous strong hand." **Isaiah 41:10 (CEB)**

<u>Get Back to Beautiful Exercise:</u> Make a list of what you are good at doing. This list must include all things that come naturally to you but more importantly, they are done with passion. For the items identified, pray about how these things can be tied to your purpose. I can tell you that in one way or another your purpose is on the list and you just need to do the work to see it through.

Believe in yourself, Anything is possible

Day #9

What are you scared of? What are your fears of loving yourself? Do you think you won't like the person that you have become? We all have something about ourselves that we don't like but I'm 100% positive that if we were honest with ourselves we would actually see that we love ourselves. We may look at our trials and tribulations and think that we are not worthy of love but let me tell you that you are **absolutely** worthy of love. God's sacrifice for us has shown that we are worthy of His love which is the greatest gift we can ever receive. Therefore, if your heavenly father can love you then why can't you love yourself? Stop being afraid of loving you!

Affirmation: I'm not afraid of loving me!

Daily Scripture: Give thanks to the Lord, for he *is* good; *his love* endures forever. **1 Chron. 16:34**

<u>Get Back to Beautiful Exercise:</u> Go back to the mirror and say, "Girl, I love you!" Say it 10 times and write what you are feeling. Let the tears fall as they come but remember that God loves you, and you love yourself. Don't think of your imperfections but focus on the love! Don't let the hurt define you! Allow God's love to define you! You are love!

Day #10

Push, push, push! Push past your fear of failing! Push past your fear of success! Push towards your victory! Push towards your goals! Push your beliefs until your dream is accomplished. You were created for a time such as this! God created you for a bigger purpose than your fears! Let go of everything that hinders you and push, push, push! You can't gain what you don't go after and you can't lose what you don't let go!

Affirmation: His love never quits so I won't either!

Daily Scripture: I have told you these things, so that in me you may have peace. In this world you will have trouble. But take heart! I have overcome the world. **John 16:33 NIV**

Get Back to Beautiful Exercise: Write a list of five things that have been prevented you from

Katrina M. Henderson

pursuing your purpose and why they have stopped you. Now, write a plan to let them go! Let them go and gain your purpose!

Day #11

Divorce is not just for the married unhappy folks! Sometimes we need to divorce our relationships (even family) because they are toxic to us living out our purpose. We think that these relationships are needed but if we can't be our true selves then we need to separate from them. We should never be trying to hold onto a relationship that stops us from living. There is a difference between when God says hold on and when we say hold on because we don't want to be alone. **Stop hanging out with people who won't bring out the best in you!**

Who said being alone is a bad thing? It's not because it allows you the opportunity to love you! It gives you the opportunity to discover what you enjoy in life. It gives you the opportunity to see your beauty for who you are and not what you do for someone else!

Have the courage and faith to step, when no one else will step with you!

Affirmation: I will live! I have the courage and faith to live my life!

<u>Daily scripture:</u> Be strong and courageous. Do not be afraid or terrified because of them, for the LORD your God goes with you; he will never leave you nor forsake you. **Deuteronomy 31:6 NIV**

<u>Get Back to Beautiful Exercise:</u> Write a list of five relationships you need to let go. Pray about them and ask God for the strength to let them go. Don't be afraid of being alone because God is with you every step of the way.

STOP looking for closure from people you should have never been open to in the first place. They left because they weren't purposed to stay! God has a plan for your life and some people are in your life but only for a season.

Day #12

How do you handle the stresses of life? How do you find relief for those difficult moments when it seems like you have nothing left? Pray? Cry? Dance? No matter what challenges come your way, your strength is found in holding on. I know it seems difficult to hold on when it seems like no options are available for the situation but trust me it will get better. Challenges come to show us the need to lean on someone higher than us -- God! God has already paid the price for us. He gives us the strength to get through. We just have to call Him for the strength to see the rainbow on the other side. God's comfort provides what we need. He's waiting on you to let it all go and turn to Him for comfort. Only He can give you the answers for which you are looking! Only He can lift the burden or heaviness you feel! You will see that you are stronger than you could have ever imagined because it's during those moments we trade our weakness for God's strength!

Affirmation: I am a survivor!

<u>Daily scripture:</u>   Yet what we suffer now is nothing compared to the glory he will reveal to us later. **Roman 8:18 NLT**

<u>Get Back to Beautiful Exercise:</u>   Write your greatest challenge down and write why this is a challenge. Once you have written them down, find five scriptures to help you find comfort and peace in the storm. Each time you are faced with a challenge, return to these scriptures or find more. No matter what, you will make it through!

Day #13

Don't stop dreaming! Don't stop believing! I know life is hard and you are questioning why you have to go through this! Just know that there is a reason and season for everything! God does not leave us during trials because He is there carrying us through them! You may not think you have the skills you need but God says you're equipped. Continue to push through! Continue to dream! Continue to love! No matter what, just continue! I know the struggle is real but so is God! You got this! Don't stop dreaming! Don't stop believing!

Affirmation: I am strong and I do believe!

Daily scripture: But you, LORD, do not be far from me. You are my strength; come quickly to help me. **Psalm 22:19 NIV**

<u>Get Back to Beautiful Exercise:</u> Revisit the list that you made on Day 8 and write a plan to go after the top three purposes. Don't let your fears stop you from fulfilling your dreams! If you don't have the knowledge or resources, talk to some people and ask for suggestions on how to get what you need. Maybe, you need to take classes, find a mentor, or just be connected to other people who've been where you are! Continue dreaming! Continue believing! You are stronger than you think!

Day #14

How many times have we sat and had a pity party because something hasn't gone our way? We think we put so much effort into it, but we never sit back and reflect on what could have been done differently. Did you really give it your all? Did you really have the right spirit going into it? Did you really go into it with expectancy thinking this job is mine? Did you visualize yourself walking it out?

Beautiful, you have to keep moving forward! You have to continue pushing through despite the no! You have to continue living! Don't let God's denial of things stop you from pursuing! Did you ever think that He didn't allow that door to open because He has something bigger and better in store for you? Perhaps, you weren't really ready for it! Whatever the no, praise God for it because He's protected you from it. **God is with you every step of the way so breathe and praise him all the way through it!**

Affirmation: I walk with expectancy!

Daily scripture: Why are you cast down, O my soul? And why are you disquieted within me? Hope in God; for I shall yet praise Him, the help of my countenance and my God. **Psalm 42:11 NKJV**

Get Back to Beautiful Exercise: Write down a list of at least five things that didn't go your way. Next to each of those things, really reflect on why you think there was a "no". Do you need more training? Do you need more finances? Do you need to let go of some relationships? Or, do you need more faith? Whatever the reason, go to God in prayer and have Him clarify the "no".

Day #15

Have you let your finances stop you from pursuing your purpose? Do you live from paycheck to paycheck and wonder how you could ever start your own business or follow your dream? Well, do you have a budget? Careful planning and budgeting allow you to see areas in your spending that need changing! If you stopped eating out for lunch and brought your lunch, you will see savings. If you cut back the cable, you will see savings! If you sacrificed that new outfit and just found a way to mix things up, you will see savings! Owning a business or pursuing your purpose is all about making a sacrifice and investing in yourself!

Affirmation: I am prosperous!

Daily scripture: And my God will supply all your needs according to His riches in glory in Christ Jesus. **Philippians 4:19 ESV**

<u>Get Back to Beautiful Exercise:</u> Make a list of all your expenses and divide those expenses into two groups: 1) "Must Have" which would be items like food (cooking not take out), transportation costs, rent, etc., and 2) "Wants" which would include spa day, movies, dinner out, etc. For the items that are determined as "wants", really decide on whether you can make the sacrifice and skip it for the month. If so, take that money and invest it in some new resources such as a class, business books, coaching, or mentorship. Anything that will help you expand your mindset and gets you to focus on pursuing your purpose. For those items identified as "must have", really evaluate whether they are a must have. Perhaps, you need to downsize your house or maybe you could take the train to work rather than drive! You may identify some "musts" that are really "needs" and can be invested into your purpose.

Commit to these sacrifices for at least six months and watch your finances grow!

Day #16

As a mom, I am wondering whether I'm raising my kids the way God would have me to raise them. Am I too overprotective? Did I not discipline my oldest enough because I was trying to be her friend? Am I allowing my two youngest more freedoms because I'm recognizing the importance of life? Whatever the situation, we as mothers do the best we can and we have to accept that! There is no instruction manual and we do what we do from experience. Some of us are raising our children in a particular way because we have made a vow to ourselves that "I won't do like so and so did." Then some of us do what we do because we are so frustrated with life that we just don't care. No matter what our reasons were, or what journey we took to get to the point of where we are, being a mother is a great gift! **The process of being a mother can be a struggle but the process is so worth it when you see the smiles of the little ones.** We just have to learn to forgive ourselves and pray that our children will one day understand that we are imperfect people too!

Affirmation: I will forgive imperfect people including myself!

<u>Daily scripture:</u> But you, LORD, do not be far from me. You are my strength; come quickly to help me. **Ephesians 4:2**

<u>Get Back to Beautiful Exercise:</u> Get into a quiet space and write a letter to yourself. The person that you are writing to is the child within you not the adult that you are. Explain how your fears and hurt were not because of you as an adult; rather those fears and hurts came because of imperfect people and that it's ok to forgive. You only did the best you could so tell the adult that you forgive her! Release every burden that you carried as an adult, because you only did what you knew how to do. It's time to heal and forgive you and anyone else for the hurt and pain that you've felt! Your beauty is in the forgiveness!

If you are not a mother then reflect on a time during your childhood and write a letter to yourself from one or both of your parents! Offer them the opportunity to give you the apology that you needed but never got!

Hey Beautiful!
PUSh ThROUGh
You're Stronger than you think

Day #17

How many times have we felt overwhelmed because of what's on our plates? We think we can handle it all and never want to say "no." We get concerned about hurting someone's feeling because we don't want to say "no." We take on more projects than our schedule will allow. We try to manage it all but know we are so overwhelmed. Start saying "no" but say the "no" without explanation. Your "no" does not have to explained! You do not have to explain why you are putting yourself first. Now, say it with me "NO! And no explanation is necessary."

Affirmation: No, And No Explanation is Necessary!

Daily scripture: "All you need to say is simply 'Yes' or 'No'; anything beyond this comes from the evil one." **Matthew 5:37 NIV**

<u>Get Back to Beautiful Exercise:</u> Write a list of everything you have committed to this past week. For this list, decide which items are your priorities versus request from others. For the requests from others, determine which ones are not beneficial to you and your purpose or growing your business. Consider things that are necessary for your job, but only to the extent that it doesn't truly overwhelm you. Evaluate your list and decide on whether you need to have a "real" conversation about your tasks. If the tasks are necessary, then prioritize them based on need and due date. Get your tasks done based on priority! For those things that are not necessary, pray and the find the words to say "no" to whomever made the request. Put "you" first by saying "no."

Nothing is more beautiful than the confidence in saying "no" because you put you first!

Day #18

Reality Check Time!!!

You're looking at your circumstances questioning God and having a pity party (again) because things have not gone your way! You say why me, I can't do this anymore and you are just ready to give up. Well guess what, SHUT UP AND PRAY or STOP WHINING AND PRAY! Of course, we have moments, but it's during the challenging times that we have to be still and call on God. His sacrifice has already paid the price so we need to lean on Him for the strength to overcome. Beautiful, I know it's hard and I know it's overwhelming but you have to hold on! Do not let your fears or inhibitions stop you from doing what you desire. Your breakthrough is on the other side of the trial! Push, push, push! But, SHUT UP AND PRAY or STOP WHINING AND PRAY!

Affirmation: I walk in freedom and beauty!

<u>Daily scripture:</u> Be still and know that I am God! **Psalm 46:10 NLT**

<u>Get Back to Beautiful Exercise:</u> Quiet your mind, reflect and journal on those challenges! Pray to God to lift the burden of the heaviness you feel. Leave it all right there on the paper! Our God will provide the comfort! You just need to call on Him in prayer and allow the release to take place! Let the control go and surrender to gain your freedom and beauty!

Day #19

Hey, hey, hey! How are you feeling on this journey? Tired, hurt, empowered, or determined? You probably feel a lot of emotions but I'm so proud of you for staying the course! I know it's not easy letting go of past experiences when truth is revealed, but it can be so rewarding when you see the freedom you now have. So, go on girl and get your praise on! Thank God for the victories! Thank Him for the defeats! Thank Him at all times! Praise is your weapon! Praise and giving thanks takes the "you" out of the situation and puts God in it! Praise is beautiful! Praise gives peace!

Affirmation: Beauty is in my praise!

Daily scripture: I will praise the LORD God with a song and a thankful heart." **Psalm 69:30 CEV**

Get Back to Beautiful Exercise: For this exercise, you are going to need paper, a jar, and a heart of thanksgiving! You are going to create a gratitude jar!

Tear the paper into smaller pieces that will allow you to write down messages of thanks! Fold them in half and put them inside the jar. Each moment that you feel overwhelmed pull out one of those messages, read it, and praise God for it! I can guarantee that you will have a mindset shift. When we give thanks during the moments of trial, then we find our peace!

Try adding to the jar every day and revisit it on December 31st when you set your goals for the New Year. Reflect on the good God has done and get ready for the ride! Praise and giving thanks changes your perspective! Beauty is in your praise!

Just remember that when setting your goals, always check in and make sure they line up with the master plan!

Day #20

Boom, Pow, Ouch! Life comes at us and we believe we are supposed to keep going! We take everything thrown at us and say I'll be ok. But on the inside, we are dying because we are unhappy and have given up on ourselves. We think we have to do it all and be there for everyone. Don't get me wrong, God gives us the power to endure but we also have to evaluate our circumstances and determine how we played a part in things.

Stop allowing life, circumstances and even family to have so much power over us that we lose ourselves in the process! I know you want to be there for everyone, but think about the cost. You can't give someone else more power over your life than what you have yourself. Make the decision to be happy and live your life for you and only you!

<u>Affirmation</u>: I'm taking back my power! I will not let people or things have more control over my life than I do.

<u>Daily scripture:</u> The Lord will fight for you; you need to only be still. **Exodus 14:14 NIV**

<u>Get Back to Beautiful Exercise:</u> Go back to the exercise on Day 11 and review your list of five relationships you needed to let go. Did you? If you did, how do you feel? Prayerfully, you feel more confident and free because you are out of the negative relationships. Now, review your relationships and determine if there are more that you need to be let go. If so, make a list of five more. Remember, God is with you every step of the way.

If you didn't let go of those relationships, what stopped you? If you were afraid then go into prayer right now and ask for the strength to let go. Allow God to give you the courage to move on. Try again and let those five go!

Day #21

Do you have dream killers in your life? You know who they are! They never support your dreams and aspirations; they say they do but their actions tell a different story! There is nothing harder than having a vision or purpose and you're working hard towards it but feel like you're alone in your journey! Sometimes having no one can be harder than having a hater in your corner because at least the hater is pushing you to greatness. When you feel alone, you may lose the desire to keep moving forward.

However, beautiful, you can't stop pushing! Don't think about the person who's not there supporting you but focus on the person who needs you while you're fulfilling your purpose. Your life is a testimony for someone else so become your biggest cheerleader. You can be the one cheering you onto the finish line! Beautiful, you can do it! Keep pushing for the beauty at the end of your journey!

<u>Affirmation:</u> I'm my biggest cheerleader! Nothing or no one can stop me from fulfilling my purpose!

<u>Scripture:</u> But my mouth would encourage you; comfort from my lips would bring you relief. **Job 16:5 NIV**

<u>Get Back to Beautiful Exercise:</u> Stand back in front of the mirror (yes, again) and begin speaking life into your situation! Talk to yourself as if you were encouraging your best friend! Use those same words of encouragement for her and speak that over your life! Use the same tone that you would give her, if she were having a pity party and you needed to bring her out! Encourage yourself and watch your confidence fly! Be your own best friend! Be your biggest cheerleader!

Day #22

Do you know anyone who has suffered from depression or perhaps you've had moments of depression? It's a hard thing to talk about. Trust and believe that you are not alone! Everyone has experienced depression at some point in their life and some still struggle with it. No matter what, it's important to know that you are never alone. The key to overcoming it is changing your perspective on what's causing the depression. Perhaps, you have lost a family member you had a very close relationship with or maybe, your family has had some financial or other hardships. Whatever the reason, it is crucial to be honest about your feelings and speak with someone who you trust so that you can find a way to see things differently. The key is just opening up, talking about it and changing your perspective! You have to find a way to change the negative outlook into something positive!

You are not alone and you will get through this! No matter what goes on in your life, please make sure you are pressing forward and believing the best out of every situation. Be encouraged and know we have all gone through something at some point but we made it through and so will you!

<u>Affirmation:</u> I am a Survivor and I will overcome.

<u>Daily Scripture:</u> I press toward the mark for the prize of the high calling of God in Christ Jesus. **Philippians 3:14 NIV**

<u>Get Back to Beautiful Exercise:</u> Journalize what you are feeling! Be honest with God about the situation and write what you hear. Write about the hurt, write about the pain, just write! Once you have written your feelings, release them to God and begin praising Him for any and every situation! Praise Him for the good and the bad! Praise Him for the pain! Praise him for the blessings! Praise Him for the trial! Let the praise shift your mindset so that you no longer look at the situation as negative, but an opportunity to draw closer to your Father. Let the pain push you into a relationship with Him!

Day #23

Let's talk about insecurity and why you need to be secure in who you are. I know you don't want me preaching to you, but can I have a real moment of vulnerability with you?

I grew up in a single-mother household with my sister. Sure, my dad was around, but he wasn't in the home with us and so there was always an emptiness within me because my first love was not in my life every day. Please don't get me wrong, my mother did a great job raising two beautiful daughters on her own. However, there was something about needing my Daddy that I longed for. If you were like me, you wanted him to tell you he loved you so much, you were beautiful, and that you could conquer the world! A father does some things that no mother can do. I can't describe it, but I know I desired to fill a void I had within my heart. So, I searched for someone to love me and fill the void by getting into relationships in hopes of feeling loved. For the longest times, these relationships just left me feeling insecure because I still didn't feel adequate to deserve their love. (Ha, if that's what you actually call it at the time! Who really knew?) During that time, I didn't have a real relationship with God to understand that I was deserving and adequate as I was. I often felt I wasn't pretty enough, or the right shape, or didn't do so and so. Whatever the idea, I had insecurities and they often interfered with my relationships because I didn't trust anyone. I wouldn't let anyone get close enough to know me for fear of getting hurt. It wasn't until I began a journey of self-discovery and realized who I actually was by seeing myself as God saw me. Studying the Bible helped me understand that I was a gift, God loved me unconditionally, and that was the greatest love of all!

So, beautiful, stop living for others and begin living for yourself! Stop thinking that you are inadequate and walk in the security of knowing God loves you with your flaws and all! Be secure in who He created and know that He made you just the way you are!

Affirmation: God's love for me is the greatest love of all! Today and every day, I choose His love!

Daily Scripture: But the Lord has become my fortress and my God my rock in whom I take refuge. **Psalm 94:22 NIV**

Get Back to Beautiful Exercise: Stand in a mirror and repeat after me, "This is what God's love looks like." Repeat this 10 times until you feel the insecurity leave your body. I know it sounds crazy but trust me. When you hear your voice saying the words and start believing in your heart then you will understand you are loved and you have nothing else to prove to anyone else.

Day #24

If others see your greatness, why won't you? We are always more critical of ourselves which causes us to hesitate to carry out our dreams. We think negatively and say we can't do it and we stop trying! We won't have enough confidence to walk out the purpose God has created us for because of our fear of failing. But beautiful, I am here to tell you that you have gifts someone else needs! God created us all with a purpose and we must walk in our faith and carry that purpose out! Stop letting the fear of people or failure stop you from trying! If you never try then how do you know you can't do it! Yes, we may not succeed but at least we tried. We learned from our lessons on what to do differently so we have another opportunity to try again! Let your fear of not helping someone else with your gifts push you past the fear! Let your faith in God push you towards the purpose!

Be the person God created you to be and don't be afraid to try!

Affirmation: I won't be scared to try because God created the beautiful person that I am.

Daily Scripture: May he give you the desire of your heart and make all your plans succeed **2 Chronicles 15:7 NIV**

Get Back to Beautiful Exercise: Go back to Day 13 and narrow it down to one purpose. For this purpose, make a list of five things needed to fulfill the list and create action steps or research resources to help you accomplish those things. Make a commitment to yourself to move forward in your purpose.

Day #25

Let's talk about power and control! As women, we tend to be the ones consistently giving to others and sacrificing our dreams and aspirations! We feel like if we can just help others with their needs, then things would be all right. Little do we know that we have now become the enabler and they never stop looking for us to save the day!

If you are like me, you have a hard time saying 'no' because you don't want to hurt anyone's feelings or think that if I don't do it then who will! There we go, trying to be wonder woman again! From my own attempts of doing for others, I sacrificed myself. I gave more to others than what I was willing to give myself. As a result, I was hurting, burnt out, and I needed to find another way!

Think about it this way, would you work your job for 24 hours straight if you were asked? You are dead tired so you would politely say 'no,' however, in your mind you are screaming some not-so-choice words and wondering why they were crazy enough to ask you! Ha-ha-ha! Well if you would say 'no' to a job that puts money in your pocket, why don't you say 'no' to your family and friends who require more of you than what you have to give?

Stop giving people your power! Start telling loved ones 'no' so they start doing things for themselves. More importantly, you start doing things for yourself! Take your power back and feel the freedom that comes from taking care of you!

Affirmation: My freedom comes from me putting myself first. I'm taking my power back.

Daily Scripture: God is our refuge and strength, an ever-present help in trouble. **Psalm 46:1 NIV**

<u>Get Back to Beautiful Exercise:</u> Get two sheets of paper to create a collage. On one sheet of paper, write the word **NO** in big bold letters, and on the other write the word **YES** in big bold letters. Now, write, draw or print pictures, words or statements that you will say 'no' to and put those on the **NO** sheet. Then write, draw or print pictures, words or statements that you will say 'yes' to and put those on the **YES** sheet. Hang both lists in a visible spot and when you see it; continually say what you will say **NO** to, and what you will say **YES** to. This will help you realize that 'no' is more than a word but an actual complete sentence.

Day #26

One morning during my devotion time, I read Job 1. I've heard the story many times and probably read it as many times as well, but that day it really hit me. My initial reaction was why God would allow this to happen to His child. Like many of us, we see the storms of life and the different tragedies then we question God. We wonder 'why me' or why are certain things happening around us. In the scripture, Job loses everything he loved. And what does he do? He shaves his head, falls to his knees, and begins to worship! Yes, I said worship!

Job's trust and belief in God was so strong that he began to worship God. Then it hit me, how is my worship in times of trouble? Would I still serve God when all things are breaking loose around me?

Can I have an honest moment with you? I would have my moment of "why me" or I'd question God, but I have come to understand that I serve a greater purpose and I must see

God's will for my life fulfilled. No matter what the storm looks like, I'm pressing through because I know God's will for my life is so much greater than my feelings, my fear, and my complaints.

Therefore, you keep pushing through to purpose! Keep smiling and don't let the circumstances steal the beauty within!

Affirmation: I am more than a conqueror!

Daily Scripture: No, in all these things we are *more than* conquerors through him who loved us. **Romans 8:37 NIV**

<u>Get Back to Beautiful Exercise:</u> Read Job 1 and see what he experienced. Reflect and journal on what God reveals to you about his journey. Think about the worst things you've experienced and start praying and believing God for the victory! If you are reading this, then you are still standing and those tests and trials have become your testimony. Now, share your story!

Day #27

It's 7:39 pm and you are just getting in from work. As soon as we walk in the door, some of us have running, screaming kids, and a barking dog. As you mindfully maneuver your way through the Legos and crayons scattered everywhere, you feel like hell is breaking loose because your house is a mess! However, it's not. It's just the way children explore the world and walk in their freedom. They get bored so quickly or easily distracted that they don't realize the importance of cleaning up because they are too busy living in the moment.

Do not let what feels like chaos throw you for a loop! Learn to enjoy the moment and get down and play with them. Don't let the mess cause you to feel depressed because you don't have it all together. Be thankful for your little ones and appreciate the time you have with them. They won't be little for long, so appreciate the moment. Appreciate the creativity that God placed in them! Pray for God to give you the patience and peace to enjoy life! Stop worrying about the house and live!

Affirmation: Being a mom is a wonderful thing! I will not take each day for granted. I will live in the moment.

Daily Scripture: Be joyful in hope, patient in affliction, faithful in prayer **Romans 12:12 NIV**

Get Back to Beautiful Exercise: The next time you come home, drop all your things and run to your children. Join or initiate playtime with them and enjoy the moment. Don't let the worry of dinner, cleaning or work interrupt one moment with them. Once they are down for the night, come back and journalize on how you felt playing with them. When the moments get tough, reflect on those beautiful smiles from this playful night as those are the memories that get you through.

Day #28

In September, my husband and I celebrated six years of marriage. We are so thankful for our journey but we realized that we needed time for us so we went away for the weekend. During our weekend, we talked about what we needed more from each other. It was a time for us. During our dating years, we managed to have date nights or days. However, after the kids were born, now we fill those days and nights with sports and activities for them. We kind of just shifted our focus to the kids, but never realized the importance of taking time for us.

So, let me ask you, when was the last time you and your spouse took time for you as a couple? Spending time together allows you to connect without the distractions of little ones, big ones and life in general. It's about disconnecting from the hustle and bustle of life and reconnecting as a couple. Taking time for you as a couple helps to appreciate one another and reminds each of you of the love you have. So, take the time for each other as a couple!

Affirmation: I am committed to my marriage and I will take time for us!

Daily Scripture: And let us consider how we may spur one another on toward love and good deeds, not giving up meeting together, as some are in the habit of doing, but encouraging one another—and all the more as you see the day approaching. **Hebrews 10:24-25 NIV**

Get Back to Beautiful Exercise: Talk with your spouse about how you can get away and take time for each other. Figure out where you can go to just talk and reconnect. While away, each of you take some time to talk about what you need from each other. Don't take this time to nag about what each other is doing wrong, but talk about how you can take your relationship to another level. Make this about going forward together not exploring what you or he can be doing differently! Be honest about what you need and just listen to him explain what he needs. Then make a plan to move forward with accomplishing those needs. Finally, make a commitment to be alone together as least once every other month!

MR MRS

Day #29

God, I thank you for this beautiful one who has changed her perspective on her life and realized her beauty and purpose! I thank you for her journey and pray that You continue to give her healing for any hurt she may have felt! I pray that You continue covering her and reassuring her that You never left her side and that You will never leave her side! I pray that You continue whispering to her and confirming the greatness You created within her! She held on, and I pray she is restored! AMEN

Sweet love, you are almost there! You said yes to yourself and let the distractions go! I know they may not be gone forever, but you now have some encouragement and tools that can help when they try to get you off course!

Affirmation: I can do it!

<u>Daily scripture:</u> In him and through faith in him we may approach God with freedom and confidence. **Ephesians 3:12 NIV**

<u>Get Back to Beautiful Exercise:</u> For the last 29 days, I've given you daily affirmations to help you realize the beauty within. Well, it's your turn to write your own. You've dismissed the lies that your mind told you, you found strength in the storm, you let go of control and you lived! Now, write 10 more affirmations and put them up around the house. As you walk past them, continue saying them to yourself! Don't let ever let someone else or even yourself tell you that are you anything less than beautiful! The only way to change your perspective on life, Beautiful, is to change your mindset!

Day #30

Well, you made it! Although we may have never met, I'm so very proud of you! God came through like he always does! And, this deserves a praise party!

You may have been nervous or hesitant to do the work because of the vulnerability that you had to have in order to discover your beauty! But, you stayed the course despite the hurt that you may have identified. Now that you know and believe you are **truly** beautiful, don't stop here! Don't let this journey of loving you and accepting that you are beautiful end! Continue pushing forward! Continue on with your purpose! I pray that you have nothing but success and will share this journey for the next woman who needs to realize her beauty!

Congratulations, on getting your beauty back! Now, get your praise on! You deserve it, Beautiful!

Affirmation: I'm back and I am beautiful!

<u>Daily scripture:</u> Be strong and take heart, all you who hope in the LORD. **Psalm 31:24 NIV**

<u>Get Back to Beautiful Exercise:</u> Just like in Day One, stand in the mirror and say **"I am beautiful"** 10 times, and journalize what you are feeling. Compare your responses and I pray that you see the transformation that God took you through!

About the Author

Katrina Henderson is the Memories Creator of Unbreakable Memories. She has answered the call of encouraging women to see the beauty within them. She encourages women to believe they are worthy of loving themselves despite the trials and circumstances they may have encountered.

To connect with Katrina, visit
http://www.unbreakablememories.com

Stay encouraged and reminded of your beauty within!

Get your free hello beautiful affirmations at:

http://bit.ly/hellobeautifulaffirmations

CPSIA information can be obtained at www.ICGtesting.com
Printed in the USA
LVIW01n1720190818
587443LV00009B/43